MOMS

Compiled by David Baird

RONNIE
SELLERS
PRODUCTIONS

-Gift Books-

Life began with waking up
and loving my mother's face.

George Eliot

Of all the rights
of women,
the greatest is
to be a mother.

Lin Yu-tang

Happy is the son whose faith in his mother remains unchallenged.

Louisa May Alcott

My mother taught me that every night a procession of junks carrying lanterns moves silently across the sky, and the water sprinkled from their paddles falls to the earth in the form of dew.

Allen Upward

God could not be everywhere,
so he created mothers.

Jewish proverb

Who ran to help me when I fell,
And would some pretty story tell,
Or kiss the place to make it well?
My Mother.

Ann Taylor

The heart of a mother is a deep abyss at the bottom of which you will always find forgiveness.

Honoré de Balzac

You should study not only that you
become a mother when your child is born,
but also that you become a child.

Dogen

A mother's love is like an
endless box of chocolates;
you can't believe it's so good
and that it goes on forever.

Author unknown

From her humor we find joy.
From her spirit we draw confidence.
From her imagination we learn creativity.
And from her patience we learn balance.

David Butler

Every beetle is a gazelle
in the eyes of its mother.

Moorish proverb

Most of all other <u>beautiful</u> things in life come by twos and threes, by dozens and hundreds. Plenty of roses, stars, rainbows, brothers and sisters, aunts and cousins, but only one mother in the whole world.

Kate Douglas Wiggin

A man never sees all that
his mother has been to
him until it's too late to
let her know he sees it.

William Dean Howells

I wish
thee
all thy
mother's
graces…

Richard Corbet

A mother understands
what a child does not say.

Jewish proverb

Her love is like an island
In life's ocean, vast and wide,
A peaceful, quiet shelter
From the wind, and rain, and tide.
'Tis bound on the north by Hope,
By Patience on the west,
By tender Counsel on the south,
And on the east by Rest.
Above it like a beacon light
Shine faith, and truth, and prayer:
And through the changing scenes
   of life,
I find a haven there.

Author unknown

Though often contradictory in her advice, I trusted my mother totally.

Ethan Hopkins

...if there be aught surpassing
human deed or word or
thought, it is a mother's love.

Marchioness de Spadara

Thou art thy mother's glass,
  and she in thee
Calls back the lovely April
  of her prime.

William Shakespeare

Mother is the name of God in the lips and hearts of children.

William Makepeace Thackeray

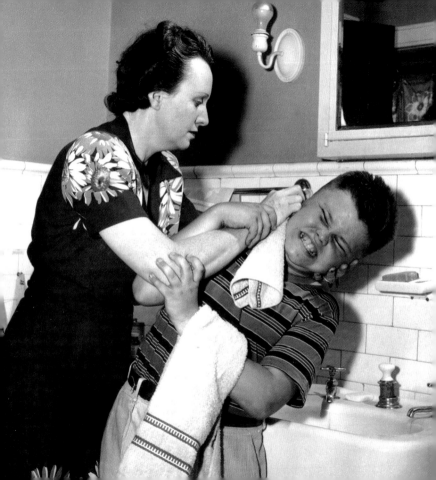

Few misfortunes can
befall a boy which bring
worse consequences
than to have a really
affectionate mother.

W. Somerset Maugham

A mother is the truest
friend we have...

Washington Irving

"If everyone jumped off a cliff, would you?" my mom used to ask me. But the saying that I remember best was "I love you."

Patricia McCann

An ounce of
mother is worth
all the flowers
in the world.

Iona Allford

Men are what
their mothers
made them.

Ralph Waldo Emerson

Who takes the
child by the hand
takes the mother
by the heart.

German saying

Thy mother a lady,
both lovely and bright.

Sir Walter Scott

No matter how
old a mother is,
she still watches
her middle-aged
children for signs
of improvement.

Florida Scott-Maxwell

My mother said to me, "If you become a soldier, you'll be a general; if you become a monk you'll end up as the pope." Instead, I became a painter and wound up as Picasso.

Pablo Picasso

Wherever mom is,
that's where home is.

Felicity Martin

What do girls do who
haven't any mothers to help
them through their troubles?

Louisa May Alcott

My mother was the most
beautiful woman I ever saw.
All I am I owe to my mother.
I attribute all my success in
life to the moral, intellectual,
and physical education I
received from her.

George Washington

Heaven is at the
feet of mothers.

Persian proverb

There is only one pretty child in the world, and every mother has it.

Chinese proverb

A man who has been the indisputable favorite of his mother keeps for life the feeling of a conqueror.

Sigmund Freud

Like mother, like daughter.

Sixteenth-century proverb

When God thought of mother he must have laughed with satisfaction and framed it quickly—so rich, so deep, so divine, so full of soul, power, and beauty, was the conception.

Henry Ward Beecher

When it comes
to love, Mom's
the word.

Anonymous

The future destiny of
the child is always the
work of the mother.

Napoleon Bonaparte

A mother is not a
person to lean on,
but a person to make
leaning unnecessary.

Dorothy Canfield Fisher

The babe at first feeds
upon the mother's
bosom, but it is
always on her heart.

Henry Ward Beecher

My mom should have been a lawyer—she always managed to persuade me that chores would be fun.

Ethan Hopkins

Motherhood:
All love begins
and ends there.

Robert Browning

35

In my interest she left no wire
unpulled, no stone unturned,
no cutlet uncooked.

Winston Churchill

The mother's heart
is the child's schoolroom.

Henry Ward Beecher

I had the most satisfactory of childhoods because Mother, small, delicate-boned, witty, and articulate, turned out to be exactly my age.

Kay Boyle

A man loves his sweetheart the most, his wife the best, but his mother the longest.

Irish saying

Education commences at the mother's knee, and every word spoken within hearsay of little children tends toward the formation of character.

Hosea Ballou

A mother's heart
is always with
her children.

Proverb

Women know
The way to rear up children, (to be just),
They know a simple, merry, tender knack
Of tying sashes, fitting baby-shoes,
And stringing pretty words that make no sense,
And kissing full sense into empty words.

Elizabeth Barrett Browning

Behind every successful man
there's a woman they call mom.

Felicity Martin

A mother is a person who seeing there are only four pieces of pie for five people, promptly announces she never did care for pie.

Tenneva Jordan

A mom holds the hands of her children for a little while but holds their hearts forever.

Author unknown

Picture Credits

All images © Getty Images, unless otherwise stated.

Text Credits

Published by Ronnie Sellers Productions, Inc.

P.O. Box 818, Portland, Maine 04104
For ordering information:
Telephone: (800) MAKE-FUN (625-3386)
Fax: (207) 772-6814
Visit our Web site: www.makefun.com
E-mail: rsp@rsvp.com

First published by MQ Publications Limited
12 The Ivories, 6-8 Northampton Street, London, United Kingdom

Copyright © MQ Publications Limited 2003

Text compilation: David Baird
Design: Philippa Jarvis

ISBN: 1-56906-514-4

Printed and bound in China.